Rastafari: The Messiah
Yehashua Son Of Makonnen

Janhoi M. Jaja

© 2017 Janhoi M. Jaja
First Edition
10 9 8 7 6 5 4 3 2 1

All rights reserved. No part of this book may be reproduced, stored in a retrieval system, or transmitted, in any form or by any means, electronic, mechanical, photocopying, recording, or otherwise, without the prior written permission of the publishers or author.

All LMH titles, imprints and distributed lines are available at special quantity discounts for bulk purchases for sales promotions, premiums, fund-raising, educational or institutional use.

Cover Design: Janhoi M. Jaja
Text Layout: Janhoi M. Jaja

Published by: LMH Publishing Limited
Suite 10-11, Sagicor Industrial Park,
7 Norman Road,
Kingston C.S.O., Jamaica
Tel: 876-938-0005
Fax: 876-759-8752
Email: lmhbookpublishing@cwjamaica.com
Website: www.lmhpublishing.com

Printed in the U.S.A.   ISBN: 978-976-8245-52-6

CATALOGUING-IN-PUBLICATION DATA AVAILABLE AT THE NATIONAL LIBRARY OF JAMAICA.

ACKNOWLEDGEMENTS

I give thanks to my Creator, Ancestors, Family and Friends.
JAH BE PRAISED
ONE LOVE

Table of Contents

Introduction

Chapter 1
The Birth of a King....................1

Chapter II
The Emergence of a Culture..........4

Chapter III
King Making..........................9

Chapter IV
The King Making Ritual..............15

Chapter V
The Orthodox Culture................21

Chapter VI
The Legend of Ethiopia..............34

Chapter VII
The King of Kings...................53

Chapter VIII
The Italian Aggression..............66

Chapter IX
The Freemasons......................76

Chapter X
The Birth of Judo Coptic............83

Chapter XI
The Chosen Ones.....................86

Chapter XII
The Messiah.........................90

Chapter XIII
The Birth of the Jamaican Rastafarians.....96

INTRODUCTION

This book is not to determine what religion or who you should worship. It is to show the spiritual and mystical thread that has connected events over the ages to bring about the culture/religion of the Rastafarians.

Mankind considers himself master of his destiny, but being a creature of the universe, certain forces exist that man has little or no control of. If one is not in tune and harmony with these forces there can be major disappointment and confusion.

Over the ages there have been struggles by various groups within mankind to oppose and shrug off foreign domination. The story of the Rastafarians is part of that struggle. The story of the man called Jesus the Christ was also the struggle of people of colour to end foreign domination. Yes he was a man of colour, Josephus the historian of that period, in his writings 'Capture of Jerusalem' describes him as:

"A man of simple appearance, mature age, dark skin, small stature...

The advent of the Rastafarians came about out of the need to end the domination of black people of the Diaspora similarly to the Jews in Babylon. The Christ/Messiah culture is the culture of the black man that has been hijacked by the Greeks/Romans, distorted, and used to enslave him. Ironically the teachings of Jesus the Christ was about freedom, independence, equal rights and justice. I will therefore attempt to link the past as it relates to Rastafarians with the present, and dispel some of the myths linked to Christianity.

1 The Birth of a King

"And one of the elders saith unto me weep not: Behold, the Lion of the tribe of Judah, The root of David, hath prevailed to open the book, And to loose the seven seals thereof." Rev. 5:5.

"And he hath on his vesture and on his thigh a name written, King of Kings and Lord of Lords." Rev. 19:16.

On July 23, 1892, a boy child, Lij Tafari Makonnen (Lij is a title given to a newborn boy child of royalty), was born in the Ethiopian royal kingdom. This child was destined to become one of the most influential figures to emerge on the African continent over the millennium. He was also central to the development of a vibrant culture/religion to greet the new millennium.

The culture of the Rastafarians

His Imperial Majesty is a direct descendant from the House of David. This came about from the recorded meeting of Solomon and Makeda (otherwise known as Sheba), Queen of the South that begat a son Menelik I who became king of Ethiopia. Ras Tafari is the only individual who has legitimate claim to the title Jehashua the Messiah (Jesus the Christ) since the crucifixion in the Bible of the man known as Jesus the Christ, son of Joseph two thousand years ago. He is the only one since David to successfully unify both pillars of the temple of JAH (church and state under one God). According to the Bible, the Jesus man attempted to do so during his period but failed in his bid and was crucified. It was noted that His younger brother James assumed both positions of the pillars, but the country was still under Roman control.

The unification of church and state was of fundamental importance to the Judeo Coptic culture in order to establish the 'Kingdom of Heaven' on earth. These were political goals, not supernatural or metaphysical ones, and not an 'after you die' situation also.

There are several so-called coincidences (I say so-called because I believe coincidences are divine interventions) and similarities between the life of Ras Tafari and the Jesus man. Both individuals came under Roman domination and both attempted to fulfill the prophecy of Ezekiel *Num. 24: 17*. The Jesus man failed to remove the Romans but Ras Tafari succeeded in overcoming and removing the Roman occupation that took place in 1935. He then went on to rule Ethiopia under a Theocratic government until 1974 when he was allegedly deposed and murdered by Mengistu Haile Mariam, a major in the Ethiopian army. To this day there is no evidence of this. His Majesty's body has never been found. The Ethiopian people eventually labeled Mengistu a tyrant and demon.

2 The Emergence of a Culture

In order to understand Messiahship and the heavenly pillars we have to go back in time. There is evidence that religious practices go back more than 20,000 years. These practices were a natural part of man's spiritual development. The question therefore arises as to how did man set about creating his god or gods.

Ancient man saw nature and the universe as a living entity. Man therefore being a creature of the universe learned from his experiences; he learned by observing his environs and the heavens. He accepted the fact that the sun plays the most important role of his existence and the moon is our closest heavenly body. They also recognize that these two celestial bodies have a profound and direct effect on the development of life on Earth. He realizes that the moon regulates life on Earth and the sun produces the energy for life to exist.

These two heavenly bodies became the mother and father of creation. Man then set about creating God in his own likened image.

The foundation for the development of civilization/religion is based on the planets/celestial bodies that man has been observing through eons of time. These planets became the foundation of our seven-day week, they also became the foundation of three great monotheistic religions: Judaism, Christianity and Islam, from which emerges a new and dynamic culture, Rastafarian! The culture of the man-God.

The seven planets, sun, moon, Mars, Mercury, Jupiter, Venus and Saturn, which all have direct effect on our daily lives represents the days of the week. The earth takes 365¼ days to orbit the sun. Known as the zodiac, this period is divided into twelve houses, and until later was represented by the same seven planets. Three other planets, Uranus, Pluto and Neptune were added at a later date. These twelve houses also represent the Twelve Tribes of Israel.

It should be noted here that in Jamaica there is an organization known as the Twelve Tribes of Israel with Levi listed as a tribe. However Levi is not a tribe, Levi is of the priestly order!

The Tribes are as follows:

Aries	-	Gad
Taurus	-	Ephraim
Gemini	-	Manasseh
Cancer	-	Issachar
Leo	-	Judah
Virgo	-	Naphtali
Libra	-	Asher
Scorpio	-	Dan
Sagittarius	-	Benjamin
Capricorn	-	Zebulon
Aquarius	-	Reuben
Pisces	-	Simeon

We also have what is known as the Sacred Trapezoid, this is the angle the earth tilts on its axis in relationship to its pole star as it orbits the sun (23 1/2 degrees). This also is influenced by the star system Trapezoids. The measurements and numbers 10 5 6 5 of the Trapezoid represents the numerical value of the Hebrew letters YHVH, the name considered by the Jews as the most sacred and ancient name of the God-Head otherwise called the Tetragrammaton, which represents the four elements of creation. Fire, water, air, earth (more on the Tetragrammaton in a later chapter).

The Judeo Coptic culture is one of the oldest religions known to man, a culture formalized by Moses who it is said to be the father of, on principles expressed as the Kabala. These principles were taken from the ancient Egyptian culture of Ma-at, which was influenced by the stars in our galaxy. This culture was also based on the principles of mathematics. It's about numbers, as John Hancock in his book *The Sign And The Seal* speaks about Saint Bernard asking the question 'What is God?' and then replying to his own rhetorical question with 'He is length, width, height and depth'.

One great mathematician Pythagoras, famous for the Pythagorean theorem, studied mysticism and was initiated into the Egyptian mystery school. The Hebrew culture/religion therefore evolved out of astronomy and astrology, the study of the heavenly bodies and their influence on life on planet Earth.

3 King Making

One of the first rituals created by man in his development as a civilized society is the selection of a leader. This leader became their king whose responsibility was to insure the productivity and protection of the community. There was also a spiritual head known as the high priest whose training from birth was to study the heavens and have knowledge of the universe. He was the one who controlled and determined all aspects of life, living in the community. This includes the dispensing of justice, land administration, scientific, theological learning and religious rituals. Sometimes this person assumes the position of king also. A special ritual was therefore developed for the ceremony of making a king.

These were secret rituals that involved only the kings and priests.

Sumer is regarded as the birthplace of civilization and has been identified by etymologists as the Garden of Eden in Genesis. It has been established that Sumer was a great civilization before and after the flood, which is estimated to have taken place about 3500 B.C. It is said that Sumer provided us with our creation story and our concept of God.

Sumer also gave to civilization the wheel, precious metals, and the alphabet among many other things such as farming and building. It also developed the concept of the heavenly pillar, a concept that runs through all ancient and archaic traditions. Christopher Lomax and Robert Knight, authors of *The Hiram Key* state:

"The concept of a pillar or holy mountain of the earth with the sky (heaven) is a Sumerian concept that has found its way into many belief systems including those of Northern Asia."

However, Sumerian and Egyptian culture seems to have developed simultaneously considering the proximity to each other. The Egyptians developed the concept of the pillars further by creating the twin heavenly pillars for the unification of Upper and Lower Egypt. This was incorporated into what was called 'the king making ritual'.

The authors go on to state:

"The building of the pyramids fulfilled the same needs for the Egyptians as the stepped Ziggurats had for the Sumerian people in that they were artificial mountains that helped the king and his priest reach up towards the gods. But far more ancient than the pyramids was the pillar which had the same function of reaching between the world of men and the world of the gods."

It was the Egyptians who gave us our first calendar and brought about the concept of the trinity with the uniting of the two lands with the twin pillars under one heaven. The authors of *The Hiram Key* continue by stating:

"Prior to the unification, each of the two lands had its principal pillar to connect the king and his priests with the gods. It seems reasonable to assume that when Upper and Lower Egypt became two kingdoms in one,

both pillars would have been retained. Each pillar was a spiritual umbilical cord between heaven and Earth, and the Egyptians needed a new theological framework to express the relationship of their new trinity of two lands, one heaven."

The development of the Jewish culture has its direct link to Sumer and Egypt. The Tree of Life is the centerpiece of the Hebrew culture and is a development of the pillar paradigm. The history of the Jews according to the Bible claims descent from Shem the son of Noah, who was himself a character from Sumerian legend. It was Abram, regarded as the father of Judaism, who left Sumer to find the promised land, sojourning first in Egypt.

The Bible states in *Genesis 12:10:*

"And it came to pass, that, when Abram was come into Egypt, the Egyptians beheld the woman that she was fair."

Abram was able to develop a distinct culture/religion 'the God of Abram' based on what was learnt in Egypt and Sumer to pass on to a wandering band of people known as the Habirus, later to be known as the Hebrews.

The Jews therefore regarded Abram as the first Christ. However, the most significant development of the Jewish culture took place with Moses, a historical figure regarded as the lawgiver and kingmaker.

Moses was raised as a member of the Egyptian royal family; he became a general in the army and a high priest. He therefore had access to the most inner secrets of the kingdom. *Acts 7:22 states:*

"Moses was learned in all the wisdom of the Egyptians."

The authors of *The Hiram Key* further states:

"By the time that Moses was involved with the Egyptian royal family, the New Kingdom would have been established and the 'substituted secrets' would have replaced the 'original secrets' of Osiris.

As a senior member of the Pharaoh's court, Moses must have been instructed in the principles of resurrection described around the legend of Seqenenre Tao and his fearless sacrifice, which replaced the lost genuine secrets. For the young Moses this ritual was to acquaint him with the secrets of king making, the highest expression of power, the mere possession of which was a mark of royalty. This must have made a deep impression upon him because he surely carried the story with him, so that it eventually became the new secret rite-of-passage for king making in the new land of Israel. Because it was secret and only passed to the smallest possible group of principal Jews, the story of the king that was lost passed on into the royal line of David without much change, the details of the Exodus were a lower level story available to everyone, and truth and fiction merged until little reality remained."

Moses, with the knowledge gained from the Egyptians, established himself as leader of the Habirus/Hebrews later to become the Jews. It must be noted the Jews are not a race, it is an amalgamation of cultures/different races. The Jews actually got their name from the tribe of Judah which gained ascendancy after Reuben the first born fell out of grace with his father Jacob. I will return to Moses in a later chapter.

4 The King Making Ritual

The wisdom of the Egyptians goes back to the ancient king making ritual of Osiris, Isis and Horus. Horus the god king received the divine right to rule, this ancient art was lost during the reign of Seqenenre Tao in a situation that has become part of modern day Freemasonry rituals. The authors of this well researched book *The Hiram Key* state:

"The rulers of Egypt, first the kings and later the Pharaohs were gods as well as men who ruled by divine right. Each king was 'the son of god' who at the point of death became at one with his father, to be god in a cosmic heaven. The story of the god Osiris tells how this cycle of gods and their sons began: The

sky goddess Nut had five children the eldest of whom was Osiris, who was himself both a man and a god. As became the norm in ancient Egypt, his sister became his consort; her name was Isis. Helped by his right hand god Thoth, he ruled the country wisely and the people prospered. However, his brother Set was jealous of Osiris' success and murdered him, severing his body into several pieces, which he cast into various parts of the Nile. Isis was distraught, especially as Osiris had produced no heir, which meant that the wickedness of Set would reward him with the right to rule. Being a resourceful goddess Isis did not give in; she had the pieces of the body of Osiris located and brought to her so that she could magically have them reassembled and breathe a last brief moment of life into her brother. She then lowers herself unto the divine phallus and the seed of Osiris entered her. With Isis now bearing his child, Osiris merged with the stars where he rules the kingdom of the dead. Isis gave birth to a son called Horus who grew up to be a prince of Egypt and later challenged his father's murderer to a duel. In the ensuing battle Horus cut off Set's testicles but lost an eye *himself. Eventually the young Horus was deemed the victor and he became the first king.*

From that time on the king was always considered to be the god Horus and at the moment of his death he became Osiris and his son the new Horus. With the unification of Upper and Lower Egypt, the principal pillars that connected the kings and priests to the gods were retained, thus bringing about the trinity of two under one heaven."

The authors go on further to state:

"The unification of the two pillars represents 'stability' and there is no doubt that describes how the Egyptians felt. As long as both pillars were intact the kingdom of the two lands would prosper. This theme of strength through the unity of two pillars was, we believe, the beginning of a concept that would be adopted in many forms by later cultures including the Jews and ultimately, Freemasonry."

The pillar paradigm of Egypt was developed within a concept called Ma-at.

Ma-at is defined in P.H. Newby: *Warrior Pharaohs:*

"What characterized Egypt was the need for order. Egyptian religious beliefs had no great ethical content but in practical matters there was a general recognition that justice was a good so fundamental that it was part of the natural order of things. Pharaoh's adjuration to the vizier on his appointment made that much clear; the use of the word Ma-at, signified something more comprehensive than fairness. Originally the word was a physical term; it meant level, ordered and symmetrical like the foundation plan of a temple. Later it came to mean righteousness, truth and justice."

These are the same principles the Christ man defended in his struggle against the Romans. In ancient times Ma-at became a basis for the legal system and soon came to stand for all 'rightness', from the equilibrium of the universe and all heavenly bodies to honesty and fair dealings in daily life. Ma-at also became the hallmark of a good king and ancient records show that every king and pharaoh was described as 'he that does Ma-at', 'protector of Ma-at' or 'he that lives through Ma-at'. Social order and the balance of justice cascaded down from the fountainhead of Ma-at, from the living god Horus the king.

It is interesting to note that the word we end our prayers with, 'Amen', is an acronym of the Hebrew phrase, 'Al meleh neh eh mhan', meaning 'God is our faithful king'. You will note that many of the Pharaohs carried Amen prefixed to their name.

Ma-at was also perceived as a goddess. She was the daughter of the sun god Re, also known as Amen Re. The moon god was known as Amen Thoth.

The kingship ritual was performed secretly in the pyramids whose ceilings of the main chambers represent the sky with stars in place. Research also seems to suggest that the pyramids were to conduct initiation ceremonies for the admission of new members to the royal inner sanctum, where they were figuratively resurrected before being admitted to the 'secrets and mysteries' handed down by word of mouth from the time of the gods.

In the ceremony the king would have undergone death through a process of archaic ecstasy that has been practiced by different people for thousands and thousands of years. Mircea Eliade in her book: *Shamanism-Archaic Techniques of Ecstasy* states:

"Nowhere in the world or in history will a perfectly 'pure' and 'primordial' religious phenomenon be found." The paleoethnological and prehistoric documents at our disposition go back no further than Paleolithic; and nothing justifies the supposition that, during the hundred of thousands of years that preceded the earliest stone age, humanity did not have a religious life as intense and as various as the succeeding periods. It is almost certain that at least a part of prelithic humanity's magico-religious beliefs were preserved in later religious conceptions and mythologies. But it is also highly probable that this spiritual heritage from the prelithic period under-went continual changes as a result of the numerous cultural contacts among pre and protohistorical peoples."

5 The Orthodox Culture

It is suggested that the exodus took place shortly after the expulsion of the Hyksos. This seems to have taken place as a result of the death of Seqenenre Tao in 1570 B.C. The murder was committed because the attempt by the Hyksos king Apophis to get the secret of Horus from the Theban monarch Seqenenre Tao and priests failed. As they refused to give up the secret, they were brutally murdered as a result. Kamose the second son of Seqenenre Tao who came to power in 1570 B.C., eventually drove the Hyksos out of Egypt in 1567 B.C.

Moses, who is of Egyptian royalty, thereafter found himself in trouble with his own people. It is reported he killed an Egyptian he saw ill-treating a Habiru/Hebrew thinking no one had seen him. However, none other than a Habiru reported him to the Pharaoh, so he became a fugitive.

As the Bible records, Moses went over to Sinai in the land of the Midianites. There he met Reuel a priest of Midian who gave Zipporah his daughter to Moses in marriage. It also stated that Moses tended the flocks of Jethro his father-in-law who seems to have been the high priest. Moses spent the next 40 years developing the knowledge he brought with him from Egypt coupled with the culture of the Midianites to perfect the culture we today know as Judaism. Moses became a very powerful magician and high priest who had enough time to perfect his art; the Bible speaks of many magical feats he has performed.

During his sojourn, Moses was commissioned by his God Yahweh (YHVH) at the burning bush by the God name Eh- heh-yeh to go into Egypt to free the Hebrews. Eh-heh-yeh means 'I am' or 'I shall be'.

Exodus 3:13-14 states:

"And Moses said unto God, behold when I come unto the children of Israel, and shall say

unto them, the God of your fathers hath sent me unto you; and they shall say to me, what is his name? What shall I say unto them? And God said unto Moses 'Eh- heh-yeh ah share Eh-heh-yeh' meaning 'I am that I am' or 'I shall be that I shall be'.

It is said that Moses with his powers constantly developing, went into Egypt and brought the Children of Israel out amidst many feats of magic, including the parting of the Red Sea and plagues being unleashed on Egypt. He took the people to Midian and it was on top of Mount Sinai that Moses finally perfected his magical art at the highest level.

He created two tablets of stone purported to have been given to him on top of Mount Sinai by his God Yahweh. These tablets of stone was his symbol of supreme authority, he became the lawgiver.

He then set about establishing a new governmental order with his own brand of religion. This is what the authors of *The Hiram Key* has to say:

"Whatever route taken, the Biblical story of the Exodus clearly demonstrates that the *group led by Moses was highly Egyptianised and the worship of Egyptian deities was normal practice. Moses receiving the Ten Commandments on tablets of stone was absolutely necessary to mark the establishment of a new state. Every king had to be given his 'royal charter' from the gods as proof that he was fit to lead and that there was a basis for law and order in the new society. These tablets could only have been written in Egyptian hieroglyphics, as Moses would not have understood any other script. Because today we rely on the written word on a daily basis it is difficult for us to understand how special writing was considered to be in the second millennium BC. The idea of messages materializing out of marks on stone amazed ordinary people and the scribes who could make 'stone talk' were considered to be holders of great magic. This is easily appreciated when one realizes that the Egyptians called hieroglyphics 'the word of God' a term that would often be repeated throughout the Bible."*

The god name Yahweh is a principle of the Kabalah. These concepts and principles of the Kabalah seem to have been perfected by Moses.

Donald Michael Kraig in his book *Modern Magick* states:

> "The Kabalah was called the 'Jews Immortal Spirit' and the wise were advised to meditate upon it."

He goes on further to state:

> "The true Kabalah was an oral secret tradition which for thousands of years was jealously guarded from the profane, little is known as to where the Kabalah actually originated. There do seem to be elements of ancient Chaldean, Egyptian and even pre-Arian Indian mysticism as well as elements drawn from other less well-known Semitic peoples hidden in its depths.
>
> (It) is not a single book of simple mystical idea, it is a whole system of mystical thought and action. It is the mystical underpinnings of Judaism, Christianity and (to a lesser extent) Islam."

It has been proven that the original set of books that made up the Bible were twenty-two books, which represents the twenty-two major arcane cards of the tarot. Which also represent the twenty-two paths on the Tree of Life. The

Tree of Life is the heart of the Kabalah and is the blueprint of Moses' magical art.

Moses went on to create the ultimate symbol of religious supremacy, the Ark of the Covenant. The Ark is an Egyptian concept that Moses borrowed. As stated before Moses was a magician par-excellence. John Hancock in his book *The Sign and the Seal* states:

"Philo the respected Jewish philosopher who lived around the time of the Christ man gave a fairly detailed account of exactly what Moses was taught: Arithmetic, geometry, the lore of meters, rhythm and harmony were imparted to him by learned Egyptians. They further instructed him in the philosophy conveyed in symbols as displayed in the so-called holy 'inscriptions'. Meanwhile inhabitants of neighboring countries were assigned to teach him Assyrian letters and the Chaldean science of the heavenly bodies. This he also acquired from the Egyptians who gave special attention to Astrology."

The author goes on to state:

"Reared as an adopted son of the royal family, Moses was seen for a considerable

period as a successor to the throne. The implication of this special status I learned, was that in his youth he would have been given a thorough initiation into all the most arcane priestly secrets and into the mysteries of Egyptian magic, a course of study that would have included not only star-knowledge, as indicated by Philo, but also necromancy, divining and other aspects of occult lore."

As stated previously the Jewish religious foundation is based on Moses perfecting the principle of the Kabala, which I am led to believe. His God Yahweh (YHVH) is a creation of Moses using Kabalistic principles, and based on his background Moses was also able to create the ultimate weapon, the Ark of the Covenant! John Hancock in *The Sign and the Seal* made this observation:

'This I suspect, is what the Ark really was: a monstrous instrument capable of releasing fearful energies in an uncontrolled and catastrophic manner if it was mishandled or misused in any way, an instrument that was not conceived in the mind of God, as the Bible teaches, but rather in the mind of Moses."

The God-Head is a development using the principle of the Kabala. Donald Michael Kraig in his book *Modern Magick* explains:

"Yud-Heh-Vahv-Heh is known as the holy, ultimate and unspeakable name of God. It's true pronunciation is unknown. In English we could say that it is formed of the letters YHVH. Jews never pronounce the word, instead saying Ah-doh-nye. By placing the Hebrew vowels of Ah-doh-nye (which means 'My Lord') around the four letters, which are known as the Tetragrammaton, the word Yahovah or Jehovah is formed. Therefore, to use these 'names' show a total misunderstanding of this holy name. Yahveh or Yahweh is also a misnomer, an attempt to pronounce a word with no vowels. You see YHVH may merely be an abbreviation for a longer word or a code for other letters. It is possible that some of the letters of this name are doubled. No one knows for sure. Yud-Heh-Vahv-Heh is the English transliteration for how the Hebrew letters, represented by the YHVH, are named. The Y or Yud is said to represent archetypal masculinity (the Taoist Yang or Jungian Animus), and the first H called the Heh superior, represents archetypal

femininity (the Taoist Ying or the Jungian Anima). The V, called Vahv in Hebrew looks like an extended Yud (there is a deep magical mystery here) and represents physical masculinity, while the last H, the Heh inferior, represents physical femininity. Thus, this ultimate name of God, the Tetragrammaton, the YHVH, says that God is the ultimate unity, and perfect blend of all dualities (represented by the male – female symbolism) on all planes."

The Ark of the Covenant is the symbol of Judaism. According to the Bible it was constructed by Moses after he led the Children of Israel out of Egypt. The Ark was constructed to house the two tablets of stone with the laws given to Moses on Mount Sinai that 'Yahweh may dwell among them' on the mercy seat.

In *Exodus 25* Moses was instructed as to the exact dimensions of the Ark:

"And they shall make an Ark of shittim wood (acacia): two cubits and a half shall be the length thereof, and a cubit and a half the breadth thereof, and a cubit and a half the height thereof, (that is three feet nine inches by two feet three inches by two feet three

inches). And thou shall overlay it with pure gold within and without shall thou overlay it, and shall make upon it a crown of gold round about. And thou shall cast four rings of gold for it, and put them in the four corners thereof; and two rings shall be in the one side of it, and two rings in the other side of it. And thou shall make staves of shittim wood and overlay them with gold. And thou shall put the staves into the rings by the sides of the Ark that the Ark may be borne with them. The staves shall be in the rings of the Ark: they shall not be taken from it. And thou shall put into the Ark the testimony, which I shall give thee. And thou shall make a mercy seat of pure gold: two cubits and a half shall be the length thereof, and a cubit and a half the breadth thereof.

And thou shall make two cherubims of gold; of beaten work shall thou make them, in the two ends of the mercy seat. And make one cherub on the one end, and the other cherub on the other end: even of the mercy seat shall ye make the cherubims on the two ends thereof.

And the cherubims shall stretch forth their wings on high, covering the mercy seat with their wings, and their faces shall look one to another: toward the mercy seat shall the faces of the cherubims be. And thou shall put the mercy seat above upon the Ark, and in the Ark thou shall put the testimony that I shall give thee.

And there I will meet with thee, and I will commune with thee from above the mercy seat, from between the two cherubims, which are upon the Ark of the testimony, of all things, which I will give in commandment unto the Children of Israel."

The Ark was placed on an altar and was housed in a tent. After undergoing several ups and downs it was King David the second king of Israel who succeeded in unifying Israel and Judah under one kingdom, who was given the task of constructing a temple to house the Ark. The first seven years of his rule was from Hebron the southern land of Judah. He then went on to capture Jerusalem where he established a new capital, there he built a palace and moved the tent housing the Ark and the altar to the site where he proposed to build the Temple, a permanent house for the God Yahweh. David, who is regarded as Israel's most successful king, took Israel to heights it had never seen before. However it was Solomon his son who had the honor of building the temple for the Ark. It was also under Solomon's rule that Israel reached its highest level of grandeur.

11 Chronicles 9:22-23 states:

"And King Solomon passed all the kings of the earth in riches and wisdom. And all the kings of the earth sought the presence of Solomon to hear his wisdom, that God hath put in his heart."

Image of the Ark of the Covenant Courtesy of Peter's Scribd publication, 'The Lord of the Harvest'.

Madote

6 The Legend of Ethiopia

It was during the first decade of Solomon's reign as legend has it, that the Queen of Ethiopia visited him in Jerusalem. This event is recorded in several books including the Kebra Negast and the Bible.

The Kebra Negast records:

"And she arrived in Jerusalem, and brought to the king many precious gifts which he desired to possess greatly. And he paid her great honor and rejoiced, and he gave her an habitation in the royal palace near him."

As the story goes in the Kebra Negast: There was a man by the name of Tamrin, a merchant who worked for Makeda the Queen of Sheba. He was requested by Solomon to supply him with material for the temple he was building to house the Ark. During his visit he was greatly impressed by the wisdom, wealth and the administrative ability of Solomon.

Upon his return to Ethiopia he related to the queen about the wealth and wisdom of Solomon, and how he taught wisdom and how he directed the affairs of the kingdom based on a wise system. The queen was very impressed with what she heard about Solomon from her servant Tamrin. She therefore vowed within her heart she would go and meet this wise man she had heard such great things about. As stated before she took with her many precious gifts, which Solomon needed greatly; remember, Solomon was building the temple and needed the money.

The queen went to Jerusalem and fell in love with Solomon. The legend says:

"She saw his wisdom, his just judgments, his splendor and his grace, and heard the eloquence of his speech. She marveled in her heart and was utterly astonished in her mind, and she recognized in her understanding and perceived very clearly with her eyes how admirable he was. She wondered exceedingly because of what she saw and heard with him: how perfect he was in composure and wise in understanding, pleasant in consciousness and commanding in stature. She observed the subtlety of his voice and the discreet utterance of his lips, and that he gave his commands with dignity, and that his replies were made quietly and with the fear of God. All these things she saw, and she was astonished at the abundance of his wisdom, and there was nothing whatsoever wanting in his word and speech, but every thing that he spoke was perfect."

The queen also embraced the religion of Solomon: "From this moment I will not worship the sun, but will worship the creator of the sun, the God of Israel. And that Tabernacle of the God of Israel shall be unto me my lady and unto my seed after me, and unto all my kingdoms that are under my dominion."

Solomon himself fell in love with the queen because of her beauty and intelligence.

"She was vigorous in strength and beautiful of form, and she was undefiled in her virginity. She had reigned in her country for six years and, not withstanding her gracious attraction and her splendid form, had kept her body pure."

When she announced after six months that she was preparing to depart, Solomon pondered in his heart and said: "A woman of such splendid beauty hath come to me from the ends of the earth! What do I know? Will God give me seed in her?"

In his desire to seduce her, he tricked her. He invited the queen to an occasion to see the administration of the kingdom, and how the meals for the chosen ones of the kingdom are eaten after the manner of the righteous, and how the people are driven away after the manner of sinners.

There at the banquet "Solomon sent to her meats which would make her thirsty and drinks that were mingled with vinegar and fish and dishes made with pepper; and he gave them to the queen to eat." He invited the queen to spend the night at his palace at the end of the meal, and she said: "Swear to me by thy God, the God of Israel, that thou will not take me by force. For if I, who according to the law of men am a virgin, be seduced, I would then travel on my journey back in sorrow, affliction and tribulation."

Solomon answered and said unto her: "I swear unto thee that I will not take thee by force, but thou must also swear unto me that thou will not take by force anything that is in my house." This oath they both took and made ready for bed. Solomon said to his man servant; "Wash out the bowl and set in it a vessel of water whilst the queen is looking on, and shut the doors and go to sleep." Because of the type of meal the queen was served, it made her very thirsty. She looked to make sure that Solomon was sleeping and decided to drink of the water she had seen the servant placed in the bowl. But as she lifted the jar and was about to drink, Solomon seized her hand

and said: "Why hast thou broken the oath that thou wouldst not take by force anything that is in my house?" And she answered and said unto him in fear: "Is the oath broken by my drinking water?" And the king said unto her: "Is there anything that thou hast seen under the heavens that is more precious than water?" And the queen said: "I have sinned against myself and thou art free from thy oath. But let me drink water for my thirst." Then Solomon said unto her: "Am I then free from the oath which thou hast made me swear?" And the queen said: "Be free from thy oath, only let me drink water." And he permitted her to drink water, and after she had drunk water he worked his will with her and they slept together.

The legend continues, the queen prepared to depart and Solomon gave to her whatever her heart desire, and when she was ready to depart amidst great pomp and ceremony, Solomon took her aside and removed the ring that was on his little finger and said to her: "Take this ring so that mayest not forget me; and if it happens that I obtain seed from thee, this ring shall be unto it a sign; and if it shall be a man-child he shall come to me, and the peace of God be with thee!"

It is said that the queen reached her kingdom country called Bala Zadisareya nine months and five days after she had departed from Solomon. There she gave birth to a son named Bayna-Lehken, meaning 'son of the wise man'.

Bayna-Lehken who resembled his father in many ways, started enquiring of his father at the age of twelve. It was however not until he was twenty-two years old that he went to see his father Solomon in Jerusalem. It is said that at twenty-two years old Bayna-Lehkem was skilled in the art of war and horsemanship, in the hunting and trapping of wild beasts, and in everything that young men desired to learn. He then told his mother of his desire to go see his father and come back home.

The queen called Tamrin, the chief of her caravan and merchants and asked him to take Bayna-Lehkem to meet his father and bring him back home to assume rulership over Ethiopia. At his departure the queen took her son aside and gave him the ring Solomon had given her that he may recognize his son and might remember her words and her covenant she had made with him, that she would worship God all the days of her life, she and those who were under her dominion, with all the power God had given her.

On his way to Jerusalem, he stopped in his mother's province of Gaza. There he received honor and gifts from the people who, when they saw him marveled at the perfect likeness of Solomon. It is said that the people of Gaza to Judah were stirred up and said: "This is King Solomon". There were some who said: "The King is in Jerusalem building his house"; and others said: "This is Solomon the King, the son of David". This caused spies to go to Jerusalem to seek out the king to know what was really taking place. There they saw Solomon and told him of Bayna-Lehkem and his likeness of Solomon.

Solomon sent Benaiah the commander of his army with gifts and meat and drink to entertain the traveler, and to bring Bayna-Lehkem to him. Again great confusion when Bayna-Lehkem entered Jerusalem because of the likeness of his father: "David hath renewed his youth and hath risen from the dead."

And it is said that Solomon marveled at the likeness of Bayna-Lehkem to his father David and rose up and went into his chamber, and he arrayed his son in apparel made of cloth embroidered with gold, and a belt of gold. And he set a crown upon his head, and a ring unto his finger. Solomon then seated his son upon his throne that he might be equal in rank to himself.

When Bayna-Lehkem took the ring his mother had given him to his father in order to remind him of the reason he gave the ring to his mother, Solomon said: "Why givest thou me the ring as a sign? Without thy giving me a sign I discovered the likeness of thy form to myself, for thou art indeed my son."

Then Tamrin the merchant delivered the message from his queen; "Take this young man anoint him, consecrate and bless him, and make him king over our country, and give him the command that a woman shall never again reign in Ethiopia, and send him back in peace."

Solomon tried his best to encourage his son to stay and become king of Israel, but Bayna-Lehkem was adamant on returning to his homeland and asked that Solomon impart the knowledge and wisdom he desired, and to give him just a portion of the covering of Zion, the Tabernacle of the law of God. Solomon however kept on trying to get him to stay but to no avail; eventually Solomon allowed his son to return home.

It is said that Solomon gathered together his councilors, his officers and the elders of his kingdom, and he said unto them: "I am not able to make my son consent to dwell here. And now, hearken ye unto me and what I shall say unto you. Let us make him king of the country of Ethiopia, together with your children; ye sit on my right hand and my left hand, and in like manner the eldest of your children shall sit on his right hand and on his left hand. Ye councilors and officers, let us give him your firstborn children and we shall have two kingdoms; I will rule here with you, and our children will rule there." This represents the pillar paradigm of Egypt: two kingdoms, one God. The trinity.

Bayna-Lehkem was made king using the ancient king making ritual from Egypt. And they brought the young man into the holy of holies and he laid hold upon the horns of the altar, and sovereignty was given unto him by the mouth of Zadok the high priest, and by the mouth of Benaiah the priest, the Commander of the army of Solomon, and he anointed him with the holy oil of kingship.

Bayna-Lehkem became the Horus of David and became David II, otherwise called Menelik I, King of Ethiopia, and was given his royal charter. All the firstborns of all the nobles were appointed to be sent away to Ethiopia, including horses, chariots, riding camels, mules, wagons for carrying loads, gold, silver and splendid purple apparels, gems, pearls and precious stones.

This caused great anguish among the people; they assembled together and wept, together with their fathers and their mothers, their kinsfolk and their peoples and their countrymen. And they cursed the king secretly and reviled him because he had seized their sons against their will. Anyway they praised him and said: "Now know we that God spoke concerning thee to our father Abraham when he said:

'In thy seed shall all the nations of the earth be blessed'." And they made their faces to appear happy, and they jested before him, and they praised him exceedingly because of his wisdom. But when they said all these things unto him, he understood them in all his wisdom, and bore with them patiently, as God bareth with us patiently knowing well our sins.

And the children of the nobles of Israel, who were commanded to depart with the son of the king, took council together, saying: "What shall we do? For we must leave our country and our birthplace, and our family and the people of our city. Let us sorrow on account of our 'Lady Zion', because they are making us to leave her. For in Her they have committed us to God, and we have served Her to this day. It is because of Her and our departure that they have specially made us weep." And the others answered and said unto them: "Verily She is our Lady and our hope, and our object of boasting, and we have grown up under Her blessings. And how is it possible for us to forsake Zion our Mistress?"

Azariah the son of Zadok said to them on the oath of secrecy: "Come now, let us take with us our 'Lady Zion'. How are we to take Her? I will show you. Carry ye out my plan and if God willeth we shall be able to take our Lady with us. And if they should gain knowledge of our doing and slay us, that shall not trouble us, because we shall die for our Lady Zion."

It should be noted that the God-Head is referred to in the female gender as: 'Our Lady Zion' or 'Zion our Mistress'. This culture goes all the way into antiquity. It is the original concept of the God-Head. The woman carries the womb of creation; she is the bringer of life. When Rome took hold of the culture, male egotism caused them to change the culture to suit their culture, and then dish it out to the world under the brand name, Christianity.

It is also interesting to note that the female pillar on the Tree of Life represents, the pillar of severity. This severity is borne out by the fact that the Ark known as 'Zion our Mistress' was very severe in dealing with Her guardians and foes. In the Bible it is recorded, She took several thousand lives in some very bizarre and destructive ways.

As the legend continues, Azariah and his three brethrens, Elmeyas, Abis and Makari carried away Zion and brought it to the house of Azariah, then they went back into the house of God and they set up the frame of wood on the place where Zion had been, and covered it over with the covering of Zion, and they shut the doors and went back to their houses. After this they took lamps and set them in the place where Zion was hidden, and they sacrificed the sheep and burned offering of incense, then they spread purple cloths over it and set it in a secret place for seven days and seven nights.

David II/Menelik I blessed by his father Solomon, bade the king farewell and departed for Ethiopia; but first of all they had set Zion by night upon a chariot along with other common merchandise and stores of every sort and kind. When all the wagons were loaded, the masters of the caravan rose up and the horn was blown and the city became excited; the youths shouted loudly and awesomeness and grace crowned and surrounded Zion. They departed amidst great weeping and wailing and outcry in the city. Solomon cried with his people. When Solomon saw the majesty of those who had departed, he was deeply moved and he trembled and his bowels quaked while his tears fell drop by drop upon his apparel and he said, "Woe is me! For my glory hath departed and the crown of my splendor hath fallen. My belly is burned up because this my son hath departed, and the majesty of my city and the nobles, the children of my might, are removed. From this moment our glory hath passed away, and our kingdom hath been carried off into a strange people who know not God, even as the prophet said, 'The people who had not sought me have found me'. From this time forth the law and wisdom and understanding shall be given unto them. And my father prophesied concerning them, saying: 'Ethiopia shall stretch out her hands to God, and he shall receive her with honor, and the kings of the earth shall praise God'. And again he said: 'Behold the Philistines, and the Tyrians, and the people of Ethiopia, who were born without the law. The law shall be given unto them, and they shall call unto Zion, because of a man who shall be born. Will this man then be my son who is begotten of me?'"

Psalms 87:

Solomon gave Menelik I the covering of The Ark on his departure, this is in keeping with the wishes of the Queen. Solomon said to his son: "Take this covering of Zion, for thy mother sent a message concerning this, and had said unto thee thyself: "Give us some of the fringe of it's covering, which we can worship, so that we may not like the heathen worship another God."

On their return journey they stopped again in Gaza, his mother's province; there the people played flutes and blew horns, they beat drums and played on pipes, and the river of Egypt was moved and astonished at the sound of their songs and their rejoicing; and with them were mingled shouts and outcries of gladness, they then set out for the land of Ethiopia.

Meanwhile Solomon in his grief confided to Zadok the high priest the dream he had when the queen visited him. This caused Zadok great concern as he said: "O my Lord, why didst thou not tell me before that thou hadst seen a vision of this kind? Thou makest my knees to tremble. Woe be unto us if our sons have carried off our Lady, the holy, heavenly Zion, the Tabernacle of the Laws of God." Solomon sent him to check on Zion and when he saw that she was missing he collapsed into a dead faint. Solomon, not seeing him back for some time sent Benaiah to look for him, who came upon Zadok unconscious on the floor, and set about reviving him. When Zadok came to and looked to the place where Zion should be and was not, again fell down on the ground casting dust upon his head, then got up and went to the door and cried as he had never cried before. This got Solomon's attention and he set off in pursuit of the Ethiopians.

But Solomon never caught up with them, as the Ark used its magical powers to take them to Ethiopia. As the people of Gaza told Solomon when he asked of his son, their reply was: "He left us three days ago, and after loading their wagons none of them travelled on the ground, but their wagons were suspended in the air; they were swifter than the eagles that are in the sky, and all their baggage travelled with them in wagons above the winds." When Solomon asked if anyone had seen the Ark he was answered in the negative. He then travelled on to Egypt where he got a similar response as Gaza. It is said 'it is impossible to carry Zion away unless she wished it and Yahweh wished it.' Solomon and the elders decided therefore to keep the departure a secret.

David II the King of Ethiopia, returned to his country with joy and gladness; and marching along with their songs, their pipes and their chariots, like an army of heavenly beings, the Ethiopians arrived from Jerusalem at the city of Wakerom in a single day and they sent messengers to announce their arrival to Makeda, Queen of Ethiopia, and to report to her how they had found every good thing, and how her son had become king, and how they had brought the heavenly Zion.

The queen met her son amidst great jubilation, and on the third day of the celebrations David II was made King of Ethiopia and named Menelik I, the queen made Almeyas and Azariah the Chief of the Priests and the Chief of the Deacons and the sons of the mighty men of Israel performed the law, together with their

King David II in the Tabernacle of witness and the kingdom was made anew. The new Horus was born. David II became Menelik I. That is the legend of how the Ark arrived in Ethiopia. The historical facts are there also to verify the existence of the Ark in Ethiopia. John Hancock in his excellent book *The Sign and the Seal* has documented the factual history and travel of the Ark from Jerusalem to Ethiopia.

Makeda, Queen of Sheba, meeting Solomon
Illustration: brighamqwoolridges.blogspot.com

7 The King Of Kings

Menelik I is the first Ethiopian king from the tribe of Judah of David I, King of Jerusalem, the Solomonic dynasty. His Imperial Majesty Haile Selassie I - Ras Tafari Makonnen is the 225th descendant of that dynasty to occupy the throne of Ethiopia, City of Zion, where the Gods love to be.

It is said that Ethiopia has had the protection of the Ark to defend it from foreign domination, and was able to keep intact the ritual that was passed unto Israel by Moses from Egypt in its purest form. This ritual, which was taken into Ethiopia by Menelik I, was kept intact for almost three thousand years.

Since the departure of the Ark from Jerusalem, Israel has suffered many misfortunes that have led to the destruction of the Temple and the capture of Jerusalem between AD 67-70. A movement by a set of people known as the Essence of Qumran provided the world with a character that has dominated Christian theology for the pass two thousand years. This character came to be known as Jesus Christ, a man who according to the Greeks/Romans is the 'savior of the world'.

This is how the authors of *The Hiram Key* put it:

"The religion of Yahweh was by now coming to the attention of occultists who were fascinated by the magical properties they saw in it and who took a very different view of its meaning. The numerological elements seized their attention and even the Hebrew name of God pronounced Yahweh but was written as JHVH, took on a special meaning. The Greeks call this name of God the Tetragrammaton and treated the Jewish texts as a source of supposedly ancient esoteric wisdom. These gentiles took what they wanted from Judaism, and it was these

groups as we shall see, who were the breeding ground for a later Greek mystery cult called Christianity!"

Here now begins the distortion of the culture and the beginning of the great deception that was foisted on the world. The culture of Judaism is a culture of black people. Other Asiatic and European races assimilated into the culture and virtually took it over. This is similar to the Rastafarian movement, which now attracts various ethnic groups. It is not surprising to hear a blue-eyed Caucasian telling you they are Rastafarians, even though His Imperial Majesty is a black man.

The Jews continue to develop their culture amidst foreign domination, and it was the quest for independence that brought to prominence the man known as Jesus the Christ. It was the teaching and history of this man and his people that Greece/Rome has corrupted and served to an unsuspecting and ignorant populace.

Yehashua son of Joseph was one of the leaders of a people known as the Essenes of Qumran. This community was also bent on driving the Roman oppressors from the land considered theirs, in order to establish a theocratic system of government that was handed down to them through the ages by their forefathers. This system is to establish, 'heaven on Earth'. These people were the guardians of the Jewish faith. They were also keepers of the secret of the king making ritual. Jesus' initiation into the secret order took him three years to complete, after which he attempted to take over the leadership role.

His agenda was to have himself declared King of the Jews, also assuming the position of high priest. He then set about getting people to overthrow the foreign government that was occupying their land, and thereby unify and establish the rule of Yahweh. He was a man in a hurry, as the authors of *The Hiram Key* points out:

"As a highly intelligent man Jesus knew from the start that time was not on his side; he needed to accelerate the 'end of the age' and protect himself from the powerful enemies who had already cut down one pillar (John the Baptist). The first thing he did was to appoint some personal bodyguards to

protect him; then he followed a policy of moving around, with only brief stays in any one place. His five principal 'minders' were: James and John, whom he called 'sons of thunder': two Simons, one called 'the zealot' and the other 'the terrorist' (barjona): and as Judas 'the knifeman' (sicarius). They were no peacemakers – in Luke 22: 35-38: we are told that they inform Jesus that they already had two swords after he exorted them to sell their clothes to buy weapons."

It was during this period, the year leading up to Jesus' crucifixion that it was said that Jesus did all these miracles such as turning water into wine, the raising of Lazarus from the dead, make the blind see and so on. These expressions were just metaphors used at initiation ceremonies in the secret order. Christopher Knight and Robert Lomas explains in *The Hiram Key*:

"There clearly was a secret mystery confined to a select few amongst Jesus' followers, but until now no one has been able to explain what that secret was. We felt sure that we knew the answer, but we had to stay objective and not try and force our solution

unto the facts. Fortunately we did not have to, because the Gospels did that for us. Jesus' first miracle was to turn water into wine at the wedding at Cana. Looking at this story in the context of everything we had found out, we were certain that this was no mere conjuring bravado. It was Jesus' first attempt at recruitment outside the community, at what must have been a substantial gathering. We discovered that the term 'turning water into wine' was common parlance, equivalent to the English expression 'making a silk purse out of a sow's ear'. In this context, it really referred to Jesus using baptism to turn batches of ordinary people into those fit to enter into the 'kingdom of Heaven' in preparation for the 'end of the age'. In Qumranian terminology the uninstructed were the 'water'. Taking the phrase literally, as some less informed Christians do, is equivalent to thinking that someone had the power to turn the ears of pigs into real silk purses. The idea that Jesus went around raising a few selected people from their recent death, in a land where hundreds died daily, is another lateralization of something far more down-to-earth. The method of *making a person a member of the inner sanctum at Qumran was as we now know, the ceremony that had come down one and a half thousand years to them from Seqenenre's murder in Thebes, that had itself stemmed from the king making ceremonies of ancient Egypt going back to the fourth millennium BC. We became comfortable with the concept of the initiates being known as the 'living' and everyone else being referred to as the 'dead'."*

These same terminologies are used within the Rastafarian community. Those who see Haile Selassie I as the Christ are regarded as the conscious or 'living' one, while those outside of this knowledge are regarded as the walking 'dead'.

The Roman authorities saw this movement of the Jesus man and his followers as a threat and decided to move against them. Jesus, who represented the kingly pillar and his brother James who represented the priestly pillar, were arrested. Jesus was crucified and his brother released.

"Our earlier hypothesis that there were two Jesuses was now proven and we now *knew that the one that died was Yahashua ben Joseph – 'The King of the Jews' and his brother James, Yacob ben Joseph, was 'Jesus Barabbas' referred to that day as the 'Son of God'. We discovered the long lost speech given by James after the crucifixion in the courtyard of the Gentiles, which was twisted by later Christians to create a basis for anti-Semitism that was to last for almost two thousand years."*

Jesus' crucifixion and James' death 20 years later led to the Jewish war of AD 66 - 70 that caused the destruction of Jerusalem and the Temple of Yahweh. Thereafter began the distortion of Jesus' Nasorean teachings by the Christian Church of Rome.

"The beginning of the Christian church, we found, had nothing to do with Jesus; it was the invention of a foreigner named Saul or later Paul. We feel certain that he is the character identified in the Dead Sea Scrolls as the 'spouter of lies' and it was he who battled with James to hijack the Nasorean cult. And it was Paul and his followers who failed to understand the pillar paradigm, and trying to rationalize Jewish thinking by inventing

the peculiar and highly unJewish idea of the Holy Trinity." HK

The true teaching of Jesus the Christ is very different from what Rome doctored and gave to the world. It was about independence, freedom and kingship.

"There is a very fundamental point here which cannot be ignored: nowhere in the Old Testament does it prophesy the coming of a world savior. The Jews expected a leader to emerge who was an earthly king in the mould of David, however much Christians would like it to be so, Jesus was not the Messiah of the line of David (the Christ), because he did not succeed in becoming the undisputed king of Israel. For the Jewish people of the time, including Jesus himself there was no other meaning for the word; it is a fact of history beyond theological debate. The church is now fully aware of this misunderstanding and may claim that its early 'spiritual' interpretation of the word is true and valid, despite the fact that the Jews used the word quite differently.

However, once the church acknowledges, that the Christian and Jewish use of the term

Messiah have nothing in common it follows that the church has no right to use the Old Testament as a source of evidence regarding the coming of its Christ. To do so is barefaced fraud. We stress the point that the Jews were not expecting a god or world savior; they were simply expecting a political leader with the credentials stretching back to their first king – David."

The alteration of the culture was so complete that it led Pope Leo X who dubbed King Henry VIII 'defender of the faith' to say 'it has served us well, this myth of Christ'. *The Hiram Key* said more:

"From the fall of Jerusalem in AD70, the faith called Christianity had started to part company with its Jewish origins and soon all sight of the hero called Jehoshua was lost in foreign myths and legends. Old pagan stories were piled into a story of the man who tried to be the savior king of his people. In Rome the legend of Romulus and Remus was retold with two new lesser gods, the great saints Peter and Paul. The sun god Sol had his birthday on the 25th of December and this date was thought to be suitable for Jesus'

birthday too, so that the great gods could be celebrated on the same Feast day. The Sabbath was moved from Saturday to the sun god's day Sunday, and the symbol of the sun found its way behind the heads of the divine and the saintly in the form of the halo. The citizens of the Roman Empire found the new religion both familiar and reassuring; they might not be doing well in this life but they will get a better deal in the next. Like most people throughout history they had little use for logic, preferring to take enjoyment from the emotion of it all, asking their new (now one) God for help in times of need and praising him when things went well. Christianity became a cult of rituals rather than ideas, and theology took a back seat to political control. The Roman Empire had been a hugely successful political force, but despite its ruthless approach to holding power, its might could not last forever. It began to crumble as a cultural force, but it found that the control of the minds of the people was far more effective than just controlling their bodies. Christianity gave Rome the mechanism to establish unparalleled political might based on an unsophisticated masses who would be offered a better life after death if they did the Church's bidding." HK

Rome distorted the story of the Essences Christ man and used it for political propaganda. Constantine and his mother Helena set about corrupting a faith that was developed by Africans thousands of years ago. This they took as their own.

"Constantine above all other did a splendid job of hijacking Jewish Theology. Although he was effectively the architect of the Church he never became a Christian himself, but his mother, the Empress Helena certainly did. Helena wanted all of the Holy sites to be identified and suitably marked with a church or shrine, so she sent out teams of investigators who had instructions not to return until they had discovered every Holy location and artifact from the burning bush of Moses to the true cross itself."

They then set about destroying any evidence that might contradict their 'truth'.

"The Romanized church destroyed any evidence that portrayed its savior as a mortal rather than a god. In one of the greatest acts

of vandalism, Christians burnt the library at Alexandria in Egypt to the ground because it contained so much information about the real Jerusalem Church. In doing so they destroyed the greatest collection of ancient texts the world has ever seen. Fortunately their task proved, ultimately, impossible, as they could not remove every trace of evidence. Hence we have seen the revelations of the Gnostic Gospels and the remarkable Dead Sea Scrolls."

8 The Italian Aggression

Over the centuries that followed, Rome tried to capture and dominate Ethiopia, the southern kingdom, similarly to their quest in Jerusalem. One reason for destroying Jerusalem is the hope of finding the Ark of the Covenant and its secrets, but after realizing that it was in Ethiopia, they spared no effort in trying to conquer Ethiopia.

But because of Ethiopia's mountainous and rugged terrains it makes it difficult for one to invade and dominate them. Therefore the culture was kept intact for over three thousand years. As His Imperial Majesty says:

"Ethiopia, jealous of her freedom, has always had to struggle, both for the sake of her

territorial integrity and for the preservation of her religious liberty. The heroism, developed in the blood of our people and passed from generation to generation has served to this day as a bulwark for our freedom, so that Ethiopia has never had to bear the yoke of slavery. To this, history and the world bear witness."

Ethiopia has always been a part of the Jerusalem order. Ethiopia and Rome relation goes back to almost three thousand years, as stated in the *Kebra Negast* they are brothers:

"From the middle of Jerusalem, and from the north thereof to the southwest is the portion of the Emperor of Rome, and from the middle of Jerusalem from the north thereof to the south and to western India is the portion of the Emperor of Ethiopia. For both of them are of the seed of Shem, the sons of Noah, the seed of Abraham, the seed of David, the children of Solomon. For God gave into the seed of Shem glory because of the blessing of their father Noah. The Emperor of Rome is the son of Solomon, and the Emperor of Ethiopia is the first-born and the eldest son of Solomon."

As legend has it Bayna-Lehkem/Menelik I, 'son of the wise man', first-born of Solomon and Sheba took the original Ark of the Covenant with him when he returned to Ethiopia after spending time with his father Solomon in Jerusalem. Ethiopia therefore is the purest and last bastion of the original Jerusalem order.

Rome's mission therefore is to control Ethiopia, because Ethiopia is the only nation who can challenge Rome's authority on religion and the claim to Jesus the Christ. Over the centuries Rome has kept on trying to conquer Ethiopia culminating in the last invasion by Mussolini in 1935. It was a matter of controlling or wiping them out at any cost. His Imperial Majesty Haile Selassie I speaks at the League of Nations in 1936:

"It is not only upon warriors that the Italian government has made war. It has above all attacked populations far removed from hostilities, in order to terrorize and exterminate them. At the beginning, towards the end of 1935, Italian aircrafts hurled upon my armies bombs of teargas. Their effects were but slight. The soldiers learned to scatter,

waiting until the wind rapidly disperses the poisonous gas. The Italian aircrafts then resorted to mustard gas. Barrels of liquids were hurled upon armed groups. But this means was also not effective; the liquid affected only a few soldiers, and barrels upon the ground were themselves a warning to troops and to the population of the danger. It was at the time when the operations for the encircling of Makalle were taking place that the Italian command, fearing a rout, followed the procedure which is now my duty to denounce to the world. Special sprayers were installed on board aircrafts so that they could vaporize, over vast areas of territory, a fine, death dealing rain. Groups of nine, fifteen, eighteen aircrafts followed one another so that the fog issuing from them formed a continuous sheet. It was thus that as from the end of January 1936, soldiers, women, children, cattle, rivers, lakes and pastures were drenched continually with this deadly rain. In order to kill off systematically all living creatures, in order to more surely poison waters and pastures, the Italian command made its aircrafts pass over and over again. That was its chief method of warfare. This very refinement of barbarism consisted of carrying ravage and terror into the most densely populated parts of the territory, the points farthest removed from the scene of hostilities. The object was to scatter fear and death over a great part of the Ethiopian territory. These fearful tactics succeeded. Men and animals succumbed. The deadly rain that fell from the aircrafts made all those whom it touched fly shrieking with pain. All those who drank the poisoned water or ate the infected food also succumbed in dreadful suffering. In tens of thousands, the victims of the Italian mustard gas fell. It is in order to denounce to the civilized world the tortures inflicted upon the Ethiopian people that I resolve to come to Geneva."

It is interesting to note that throughout the aggression Rome and its consorts had the full backing of the church. Raul Valdez in *Ethiopia – The Unknown Revolution*, states:

"Mussolini got the backing of the Catholic Church, which in that period was very sympathetic to colonial interests in Africa and Asia. The Vatican hoped also that an Italian victory would lead the dissident

Coptic Church to return to the fold. Cardinal Schuter described the war as 'a national mission and a Catholic mission'."

Unlike Europeans, Africans have no desire to dominate any other race; they only want to be free to pursue their own destiny. His Imperial Majesty speaking these words also echo the sentiments of Jehashua ben Joseph in his struggle with the Romans. In fact, the community that he came from was willing to die for their independence and the preservation of their culture.

This is how the authors of *The Hiram Key* describe them prior to the destruction of Jerusalem:

"The Nasoreans who believed in the power of the sword to restore the rule of God were called Zealots and it is certain they took Jerusalem and the Temple in November, AD67 led by John of Gischala. The Zealots discovered that many of the priests of the Temple and city leaders wanted to make peace with the Romans. Such thinking was not tolerated and everyone with such views was immediately put to death. The Roman

forces were closing in all the time and it became obvious to even the most ardent Zealot that the end could not be far away. In the spring of AD68 the decision was made to hide the Temple treasures, the sacred scrolls, vessels and tithes, so that they should not fall into Gentile hands. They acted just in time, because by June the Romans destroyed Jericho and the settlement at Qumran. Two years later Jerusalem fell; Titus and the Zealots were killed or taken captive, and eventually the last of the Jews who knew the secret of the Nasoreans died when the entire population of Masada committed suicide rather than surrender to the Romans."

Haile Selassie I never lost faith in the fact that his God would never desert him. He knew he had the Ark as his protector and his personal God who traveled with him so that they became one, as did his forefather Abram:

"In Ethiopia the laying down of one's life for the sake of national independence has always been looked upon as a duty of the highest priority and has been ascribed paramount honor and value, our country has, thanks to the valor of her heroes from the

most ancient times been ever mistress of her destiny. Thus even in the dark ages through which the other nations of Africa had to pass, Ethiopia's name was well-known throughout the world because our heroic forefathers making God their shield and their defender, were able to repel in defeat and shame the enemy who descended upon her from time to time."

In his struggle to overcome his aggressors, as did his ancestors, Haile Selassie I became the conscience of the world.

"As sovereign of the Ethiopian people, I invoke this principle, for it is my duty to defend the political independence of the Ethiopian people, the territorial integrity of Ethiopia and at the same time the life, the property and liberty of each of those individuals and each of those religious or civic institutions which make up the Ethiopian people. Unhappily it is true that my people can now expect from States Members of the League of Nations no material supports. May I at least ask that the rights of my people should continue to be recognized and that, pending the moment of

Divine justice, Ethiopia may remain amongst you as the living image of violated right."

After the defeat of the Italians all the principles of Jehashua the Messiah manifested itself in the person of Ras Tafari whose faith remained steadfast in his personal God.

"Those who had attacked us rejoiced in our defeat and in our tribulation. We trusted in the Lord. He gave us victory. Our salvation is the Lord. Who here can fail to trust in God, whose judgments are all righteous and who fails not those who put their faith in him? Has not the Lord, the mightier than mighty, once again revealed that under the kingdom of heaven no one government of man is greater than the other?"

He became Jesus the Christ – Man of Compassion:

"I announced to you that I advised the Italians in Ethiopia and who were completely encircled to submit to our chiefs in order to avoid being killed. Consequently I recommend to you to receive and to keep in a suitable manner all the Italians who submit to you

with or without arms. Do not reproach them for their atrocities to which they had subjected our population. Show them that you are soldiers possessing human feelings and a human heart. Do not forget that during the battle of Adowa, the valiant Ethiopian warriors who had handed over the Italian prisoners to their emperor have increased the honor and elevated the name of Ethiopia. We recommend to you to spare their lives and treat well the enemy, which will represent humanity; we particularly recommend to you spare and respect the lives of children, women and old people. Do not pillage the goods of others, even the property of the enemy. We recommend to you not to burn any house. When I order you to respect all these things it is only to ask you to perform an act of conscience, because my heart tells me that the Ethiopian people are not unfair to any other civilized people in their respect for the laws of war."

9 The Freemasons

Since the advent of Christianity there has been a division between Christianity and Judaism, this has come about as a result of Rome's distortion of the culture, which has led the people astray, in order to assume world power. But, there is now an even more powerful body that seeks world dominion. This body is called the Freemasons.

In 1118AD a French nobleman by the name of Hugues de Payen with eight other men established an organization that was known as 'Order of the Poor Soldiers of Christ and the Temple of Solomon', later to be called the Knights Templar.

These people established their headquarters in Jerusalem on the Temple Mount in 1119AD. King Baldwin of Jerusalem supported the new order and provided them with quarters giving them exclusive use of the eastern part of the palace adjacent to the 'Dome of the Rock', which is part of the former Al-Aqsa Mosque that stood on the site of Solomon's Temple. There they worked in secret for the next seven years excavating under the Temple ruins. What were they looking for? My guess is quite simple, 'The Ark of the Covenant', which is regarded as the most priceless religious relic that existed then and now. They did not find the Ark because it was in Ethiopia, but what they found was quite valuable, because it has made them become one of the most powerful organizations that exist today. These are the same relics that were hidden by the Zealots in 68AD. One French historian, Gaetan Delaforge stated:

"The real task of the nine knights was to carry out research in the area, in order to obtain certain relics and manuscripts which contain the essence of the secret traditions of Judaism and ancient Egypt, some of which went back to the days of Moses."

These relics represented great wealth and knowledge; this knowledge became the order that white people are using today to acquire world dominion. Throughout history various governments have tried to conquer the world through various means, thus becoming the sole authority on world order. Rome in its quest for world dominion embraced the Christ religion and developed their brand of Christianity. They succeeded to an extent until they were challenged by Islam, which started in the seventh century AD.

The development of Islam by the Arabs was for the same reason that Rome embraced Christianity: world dominion through religion. Both cultures have had devastating effect on the African race. The Arabs/Muslims were the ones who started and maintained the slave trade of the Africans. The Europeans/ Christians were the ones who encouraged and took slavery to a level the world had never seen. This was the total dehumanization of a race of people.

Ethiopia is the only country in Africa that has never been conquered by external forces thus maintaining her independence for the past three thousand years. They are therefore in a position to maintain the purest form of the Judo/Coptic culture, and they were also in possession of the supreme relic, The Ark of the Covenant.

This knowledge is what took the Knights Templar to Ethiopia after they had finished excavating beneath Solomon's/Herod's Temple. They were intent on finding and stealing the Ark. Their mission however failed after King Wedem Ara – ad of Ethiopia became suspicious of their motive, and in 1306AD sent a mission to Pope Clement V at Avignon regarding their movements. John Hancock states in his book: *The Sign and the Seal:*

"It would be folly to imagine that the Ethiopian mission to Avignon in 1306 had nothing to do with the events of 1307. On the contrary it is more than probable that there was a link – and that link, I am convinced, was the Ark of the Covenant."

The Templars were a very rich and powerful organization of religious warriors; their wealth was of such that they owned huge fleets, vast amount of real estate, lots of money and a fighting force second to none. All of this was available to King Phillip IV of France. In 1185 AD the Templars apparently accompanied Prince Lalibela when he left Jerusalem and returned to Ethiopia where he deposed King Harbay and took possession of the throne. There the Templars worked along with the Ethiopians for the next hundred and odd years until the mission in 1306 AD. The subsequent inquisition and suppression of the organization on Friday, October 13th, 1307 that led to the imprisonment and crucifixion of their leader Frederick DeMolay, has made Friday the 13th a very superstitious day until this day.

However, when the round up started the main fleet of the Templars mysteriously ended up in the land in the west that came to be known as America. There are certain relics today that exist to support this fact. Christopher Knight and Robert Lomas states in their book *The Hiram Key:*

"As we were to find out in great detail later in our researches, the United States of America was created by Freemasons and it's constitution is based on Masonic principles and as we already knew, the morning star is the one that every newly raised Master

Mason is required to look towards. The star as a symbol has always been important to the United States."

The authors continue:

"They pointed their bows exactly due west and set sail on what is now the forty - second parallel in search of the land marked by the star they knew from the Nasorean scrolls was called Merica, which these French Knights referred to as 'La Merica' a name that later became simply America. They certainly landed in the Cape Cod or Rhode Island area of New England in the early weeks of 1308, setting foot on the New World nearly a century and a half before Christopher Columbus was even born. This is a strong claim, but irrefutable evidence is already in existence to show that the Templars did reach America, settled there and that they carried out journeys to and from Scotland. In the small town of Westford, Massachusetts, there is an image of a knight carved as a series of punched holes into a slab of rock. The now famous knight can be seen to be wearing a helmet and the habit of a military order and the sword shown in the weathered carving that has been identified as *having a pommelled hilt of the style of a European knight of the fourteenth century. But for us the most fascinating feature is the shield which has a clear and simple design upon it; it depicts a single masted medieval naval vessel sailing west...towards a star."*

These are the same people who control the economies and countries of America and Europe. Their mission again is world dominion in the name of Christianity. The Templars became what is known today as the Freemasons. It must be noted here that no man in America, United Kingdom, Scotland, France and certain other countries in Europe can become head of state if he is not a member of the organization. The first president of America, George Washington, and the founding fathers were all Masons.

10 The Birth Of Judo Coptic

A Syrian known as Freumentius introduced Christianity in Ethiopia in the fourth century AD. This brand of Christianity which is called Judo Coptic, is however somewhat different from Rome's adaptation. Ethiopia, with its continuous lineage, had no difficulty with the introduction because it was just an extension of what they have been practicing for three thousand years.

Ethiopia, in retaining its Judo Coptic heritage, brought about differences between themselves and Rome. There were also differences, which existed among the various religious factions within Rome. This prompted Constantine to initiate the conference of Nicea, in Turkey 20th May, 325AD. Ethiopia, however, has retained its Judo Coptic heritage to the present day, even though it has been severely challenged by Islam. Islam is another religion which seeks to dominate the world by whatever means necessary.

Islam which was developed in the seventh century AD was split into two divisions, the orthodox, who saw Mohammed their founder/prophet as the bringer of divine inspiration, and the Shiahs who saw Ali the fourth Iman, his successor, as more important. Arkon Daraul in his book *Secret Societies* states:

"From the beginning of the split in the early days of Islam, the Shiahs relied for survival upon secrecy, organization and initiation. Although the minority party in Islam, they believed that they could overcome the majority (and eventually the whole world) by superior organization and power. To this end they started a number of societies which practiced secret rites in which the personality was worshiped, and whose rank and file were trained to struggle above all for the accomplishment of world dominion."

It is the organization of the Shiah that developed the assassins and suicide killers through their leader known as Hasan, son of

Sabah, the Old Man of the Mountains. With the advent of Islam, it has sparked a crusade between Christians and Muslims in order to control the minds of the people. Osama Bin Laden states:

"It is permissible to spill their blood and take their property. God says: 'O ye who believe! Take not the Jews and the Christians for your friends and protectors: they are but friends and protectors to each other'."

Thus we see Islam from the east and western Christianity all fighting against each other to establish dominance, thus being able to impose their will on the rest of mankind. It is within this scenario that Ethiopia has maintained its culture for the past three thousand years.

11 The Chosen Ones

The question arises from time to time as to how Ethiopia has been able to remain unconquered for over three thousand years. No other country has that distinction. The reason, it is said by the people, they have been protected by the Ark, because they were the ones who, 'JAH preferred to dwell with', they were the ones willing to accept Zion in all her glory. The Ethiopians are the 'chosen ones', and it is said, 'it is impossible to carry Zion away unless she wished it, and Yahweh wished it'.

This is the culture of theocracy: with a theocratic government the king represents the God-Head in the flesh. With a righteous head you will have a righteous people, as I have stated before, the word 'Amen' we end our prayers with, simply means 'God is a faithful king'.

This brings us to the title of Jesus the Christ. Titles were always given to individuals to denote ranks in every organization. Jesus is a title derived from the Pentagrammaton. The Pentagrammaton is five letters: Y H Sh V H or Y H V Sh H, which is pronounced, Yeh- hah-shu-ah or Yeh-ho-vah-sha respectively. In Hebrew Yeh-hah-shu-ah is usually translated as Joshua, in Greek Yah-su, which in English became Jesus.

There is no name for the Supreme Being. It being 'no thing' humans can comprehend. Therefore ancient man, based on Astronomy and Mathematics, developed a system in order to define the God-Head. This system is based on the four cardinal elements of creation, earth, fire, water and air. These four elements are represented by the Tetragrammaton YHVH (letters of the Hebrew alphabet). These letters also have a numerical value of, 10 5 6 5 respectively, this is equal to 26 in numerology which represents the duality of the God-Head which is 13 + 13. The number 13 in the Hebrew alphabet represents two words, one and love, therefore the God-Head is 'One Love' (isn't this the Rastaman chant?). The number 26 is also 8 in numerology, it represents infinity – perfection. As stated before, the Tetragrammaton is the ultimate name of divinity. It signifies that the ultimate secret of God is that the Divine is the union of all dualities, male and female, both physically and spiritually.

The letter shin, which looks like three small flames, represents the flame of Divinity that is sometimes called the Holy Spirit. When the shin is placed in the middle of the Tetragrammaton you get the Pentagrammaton. Therefore the letters Yud-heh-shin-vahv-heh is a symbol representing the union of divine masculinity and femininity with physical masculinity and femininity by way of the Holy Spirit. Jesus therefore is an earthly title that anyone can hold. The word Messiah means 'a king to be', to the Greeks it became Christos, and the English translated this as Christ. Hence the word Messiah was used quite frequently in the Hebrew culture.

The Hebrew use of the title Jehashua the Messiah is their expectation of a king who would take them to a level even more glorious and prosperous than the reign of David and Solomon.

The Hebrew Alphabet with its numerical value.

12 **The Messiah**

"The purpose of life is to free the soul from the shackles of the physical body through the practice of virtue and wisdom, which would make one like a God while spending their time on earth." SL

"He who reigned on the throne of David his father was Jesus Christ, His kinsman in the flesh by a virgin, Who sat upon the throne of His God-Head; upon earth He granted to reign upon His throne the King of Ethiopia, Solomon's firstborn."

In the ancient world of Africa through to modern times, the kings were seen as men as well as gods. Each king was the 'Son of God' who ruled by 'divine right'.

His Imperial Majesty Haile Selassie I is one such king. He has been compared to Biblical characters such as David and Elijah, among others. He was described as one of the most spiritual man on earth during his time. His Christ-like qualities were shown in one of the greatest acts of compassion in modern times. This was the forgiveness of the Italians after Mussolini who invaded Ethiopia and committed many acts of atrocities, was driven out. These are the words of H.I.M. Sept. 7th, 1951, speaking to the Italians who visited him:

"We have, therefore, ever been guided and inspired by the principles of Christian charity and it was in that spirit that, from the moment of our historic return to our Empire, we called upon our faithful people to accept, respect and protect those Italians who had chosen to lead their lives among us. The thousands of your compatriots who remained here today and who participate in our national life bear testimony to the fact that this appeal has always been heard and obeyed by our people. We desire nothing but peace and the opportunity quietly and without hindrance to march along the path of progress."

Haile Selassie I has fulfilled all the tenets required to assume the title Jehashua the Messiah/Jesus the Christ. He was initiated by the ancient order; he occupied the throne for forty-four years: he is the longest reigning monarch in the history of Ethiopia. He fulfilled the prophecy of the shortest verse in the Bible, 'Jesus wept', when he arrived in Kingston, Jamaica 1966. He is the only king in modern time to be designated and proclaimed a god during his lifetime on earth. Raul Valdes Vivo in his highly critical book, *Ethiopia the Unknown Revolution*, sub title *The Country That Cut Off Its Head* admitted this fact in his sarcastic remarks:

"Up to February 1974, Ethiopians viewed Haile Selassie I as the nearest thing to a god, immune to human foibles, egoism, greed and cowardice."

He goes on further to state:

"His portrait was hung in the churches. Prayers in his honor preceded the sermons. Even phrases and actions attributed to Christ were held to be those of Haile Selassie I. Well-known German artists painted scenes depicting Christ with the poor, giving Christ

the Emperor's face, and the paintings were hung in full view. Even on altars, the Holy Trinity was supplemented by the kind, well-shaven face with half-closed eyes of the man who added the title of God's Elected to that of Emperor. In addition, official propaganda, in an effort to please all, compared him with David, King of the Hebrews."

This is the same King who was deposed on September 12th, 1974 by Mengistu Haile Mariam, a little known captain in the army, who was being called a thief, murderer, and monster! But before the end of the century it was Mengistu who was cast in the role as the true brutal monster, as depicted in several rebel posters after the demise of His Majesty. His Imperial Majesty states,

"They cannot shake the truth from its place, even if they attempt to make others believe it."

Haile Selassie I, who was vilified during and after his overthrow, has been vindicated within the passage of just two decades in time. He has proven to be the true Christ of this time.

The Psalmist in Psalms 37:37 and J.A. Rogers aptly sums up Haile Selassie I a.k.a. Rastafari:

The Psalmist:

"Mark the perfect man and behold the upright: for the end of that man is peace."

J.A. Rogers, in his book 'World's Great Men of Colour', describes Haile Selassie I as:

"Ethiopia's dauntless king, of Him it could almost be said, 'Behold the perfect man.'

Haile Selassie never once said he was God. The people proclaimed him to be. It is H.I.M. Haile Selassie I who said;

"The state is for all; religion is personal."

He went on further to define religion and spirituality:

" The temple of the Most High begins with the human body, which houses our life, the essence of our existence. Africans are in bondage today because they approach spirituality through religion provided by foreign invaders and conquerors. We must stop confusing religion and spirituality.

Religion is a set of rules, regulations and rituals created by humans, which were suppose to help people grow spiritually. Due to human imperfection religion has become corrupt, political, divisive and a tool for power struggle. Spirituality is not theology or ideology. It is simply 'a way of life, pure and original as was given by the Most High of Creation. Spirituality is a network linking us to the Most High, the universe and each other. As the essence of our existence, it embodies our culture, true identity, nationhood and destiny. A people without a nation they can really call his or her own is a people without a soul. Africa is our nation and is in spiritual and physical bondage because their leaders are turning to outside forces for solutions to African problems when everything Africa needs is within her. When African righteous people come together the world will come together. This is our destiny.

"The Egyptian theory of salvation is through a series of initiations, man has to develop his soul from the human stage to that of a god. He was expected to work out his own salvation without a mediator between himself and his God."

13 The Birth Of Jamaican Rastafarians

The culture of the Rastafarians began with the preaching of Leonard Howell, Joseph Hibbert, Archibald Dunkley and Robert Hinds in the 1930s after the coronation of His Imperial Majesty Haile Selassie I and The Empress Mennen in 1930. It grew out of the Pan African movement started by The Hon. Marcus Mosiah Garvey who is seen as a prophet among Rastafarians.

Garvey, who is a National hero of Jamaica, lived from August 17th, 1887 to June

10th, 1940. He is the founder of the UNIA–ACL, Universal Negro Improvement Association and African Communities League; he was a Pan-Africanist, Black Nationalist, publisher, journalist, entrepreneur and a great orator. The movement attracted other individuals such as Mortimer Planno, D. Mack and Fillmore Alvaranga, three people who were selected to go on a mission to Ethiopia in 1961 as part of a delegation sent by the Jamaican Government to visit the emperor. The movement gained momentum after the visit of Haile Selassie to Jamaica in 1966 and attracted such icons as Bob Marley and The Wailers who took the message of Rastafari in their music to the world and sons and daughters of the middle class.

Rastafarians is an indigenous culture of Jamaica; it's a culture of inclusion, a culture of love and respect for humanity.

IT IS THE PHILOSOPHY AND TEACHINGS OF HIS IMPERIAL MAJESTY EMPEROR HAILE SELASSIE I.

His Imperial Majesty Emperor Haile Selassie I in His speech to the League of Nations in Addis Ababa put it this way:

" Until the philosophy which holds one race superior and another inferior is finally and permanently discredited and abandoned: That until there are no longer first-class and second class citizens of any nation; That until the color of a man's skin is of no more significance than the color of his eyes; That until the basic human rights are equally guaranteed to all without regard to race; That until that day, the dream of lasting peace and world citizenship and the rule of international morality will remain but a fleeting illusion, to be pursued but never attained. Until bigotry and prejudice and malicious and inhuman self-interest have been replaced by understanding and tolerance and good-will; Until all Africans stand and speak as free beings, equal in the eyes of all men, as they are in the eyes of Heaven; Until that day, the African continent will not know peace. We Africans will fight, if necessary, and we know that we shall win, as we are confident in the victory of good over evil. We have always been religious, ever since childhood, ever since the day our father, Ras Makonnen, taught us the commandment of Our Lord the Creator. But we don't consider

our religion alone valid and have granted the people the freedom to observe any religion they please.

ONE LOVE! = JAH LOVE!

Emperor Haile Selassie I and Empress Mennen

ABOUT THE AUTHOR

Janhoi M. Jaja is 69 years old and is a Rastafarian for over 45 years. Born in Kingston, Jamaica, Janhoi grew up as the eldest of three siblings. Ever since he was a child, Janhoi Jaja was always interested in photography, religion and spirituality.

Janhoi embraced the culture of Rastafarians at around age 22 and became Jamaica's first Rastafarian photographer. He has been first in national competitions on more than one occasion, his works include album covers and public relation photos for various artistes including Bob Marley, The I Threes, Peter Tosh, Ras Michael, Ken Booth, Israel Vibration, Rastafarian Elders, Priests and many other artistes. This brought him in close contact with many Rastafarians. Janhoi's work has been published in various books and periodicals.

Being a Rastafarian, he has been constantly asked by foreigners and locals to explain the culture of Rastafarians, as there seems to be great misunderstanding regarding Haile Selassie I being the GOD-HEAD of the culture.

Talking to various people he was told that his narration of the culture has given them great overstanding (understanding). Hence the writing of this book!

ONE LOVE!

Website: www.janhoijaja.com
Email: abbajahnehoyplace@gmail.com

Bibliography

World's Great Men of Colour – J.A. Rogers

The Hiram Key – Christopher Knight and Robert Lomas

Ethiopia the Unknown Revolution/The Country That Cut off Its Head – Raul Valdes Vivo

The Sign and the Seal – Graham Hancock

Modern Magick – Donald Michael Kraig

Shamanism – Mircea Eliade

The Kebra Negast

www.ingramcontent.com/pod-product-compliance
Lightning Source LLC
Chambersburg PA
CBHW031651040426
42453CB00006B/271